Come . . . Sit in My Heart

D0711207

A Sufi Speaks His Silence

Hosain Mosavat

Copyright © 2007 by Hosain Mosavat

Front Cover photograph by Hosain Mosavat
Front Cover Design by Shekinah Errington and Judy Mosavat
Rose photographs by Hosain Mosavat
Back Cover photograph by Scott Kelby

Library of Congress Control Number: 2007902411
ISBN: Hardcover 978-1-4257-7969-6
Softcover 978-1-4257-7968-9

All rights reserved. No part of this book may be reproduced
or transmitted in any form or by any means, electronic or
mechanical, including photocopying, recording, or by any
information storage and retrieval system, without permission
in writing from the copyright owner.

This book was printed in the United States of America.

To order additional copies of this book, contact:
Xlibris Corporation
1-888-795-4274
www.Xlibris.com
Orders@Xlibris.com
39158

I dedicate this book to my Mother, who taught me music and poetry. She used to put me to sleep singing lullabies of Hafez and Rumi. Every time I write poetry, she is coming through me.

For what I have become, my dear Mother, wherever you are, I am forever grateful.

Come . . . Sit in My Heart

Hosain Mosavat

Contents

Preface

Hosain Mosavat was born and raised in Iran. He finished High School in Iran and his higher education in the United States. He came to the United States in 1955 at the age of 21. He earned his living as a public High School teacher of Math and Physics for 30 years. He's now retired and living in Whitmore Lake, Michigan.

Hosain is very giving and loving. He is sensitive to beauty, nature and his fellow humans. These are the subjects of his verse and reflect his sensitivity.

This spirituality allows him to see and feel things quickly and easily. He can compose a poem at most any time. The poetic words simply flow from his heart in a steady stream and are often recorded by his wife, Judy. The characteristics of his poetry are a true reflection of the way he lives his life every day.

The reader is in for a treat. If the reader continued for ten to fifteen minutes, the poetry casts its spell, mellowing the individual and expanding the individual's own awareness and spirituality.

This volume is well worth the reader's time.

Marshall Shearer, M.D.

Author's Biography

Born in Shiraz, Iran, 1934, where Saadi and Hafez grew up to be giants of Persian poetry. Raised in Tehran. Survived the first revolution in 1953 against the Shah. Within three days, a coup d'etat happened, financed by the CIA, which I didn't survive, because of losing fifteen friends. Also lost faith in my country. Then in 1955, with the help of my father, came to America, in which I have lived, worked and served to bring peace and harmony, trying to heal the pain and losses of my friends and my country. This book is about how far I have come from revolution to making love as a way of life. I have no regrets, only great hope for our family of mankind. No one is too small to rise and touch another soul. In the name of love and compassion, I stand before you.

Acknowledgments

Without my wife, Judy's, support, suffering, insistence and persistence, I would not have been able to do this book, and her love was the music that I wrote this poetry to.

Next, I'd like to thank Ginger Wiechers, who never gave up on helping me. And it lasted 3 years before we were able to stand up and be counted for our first book of poetry. Her hugs, smiles and, finally, financial help were the final touches of this book.

I'd also like to thank Babak Rowshan-Tabari, Mohamed Al-Azem, Doug Kramer and Mahmood Moallemian for their financial assistance that helped publish this book. I know of no poet or artist in general who can afford to publish his own book. These friends have brought me from the poorest to ecstasy. Look for them. Open your heart and you will find them.

This is a special thanks to Scott Kelby, my teacher, my master, who chased me for 3 days to photograph me. His photograph of me is on the back of this book. Scott, for the inspiration you gave me and all who love photography, we all are grateful to your mastery. There is no better way I can thank you than to say 'I love you, Scott, my Master.'

Most of all, Marshall and Peggy Shearer are responsible for me being alive. Before I faced death, I was holding Marshall's hand. When I abandoned that trip, and I opened my eyes, I was holding Marshall's hand on one side and Judy's on the other. And Judy could not have survived during that hard time without their support. And as for me, I owe my life to them. Also, thank you, Marshall, for guiding us in the path of publishing, and for your beautiful endorsement of this book.

I thank you, Shekinah Errington, for making every cell of my body move when you dance and sing and whisper to me your love and your support.

Thank you, Dan Kramer, for helping Judy. Thank you, my family of Kramers, for being there for me. And thank you, Chip Kramer, who runs the whole show, for being in touch with all who knew me during my illness. I guess Chip is the emailing king.

This is the final, final thanks to Doug Kramer, my brother, who not only financially helped, but also designed and supported a website for this book and the books that will follow. His generosity is beyond belief and his talent in music, computer skills, organization, and know-how is my greatest strength. His last comment to me was 'I feel my heart in yours.' What a thing to say to someone who loves loving. Thank you, Doug.

Also, Judy would like to thank Shekinah Errington, Jaimy Weichers, Shirley Kussner, Howard and Penny Golden, and the late Vivian Bradbury MacAlister for their guidance and support. Thank you, my friends.

And I also want to thank you all who read this book and reach out to touch in the name of love. Keep breathing fresh air within the openness of your hearts.

I have come from you
for we are born within each other
This book is written
about merging in the end
All that separates us is artificial

Just like looking at a rose:
Every eye
no matter what color, race, creed or religion
whether poor, rich, Pope or Prophet
will see the same beauty and intensity in that rose

And to me
that rose is the source of our lives
That is what brings us together
That is where we come from
and that is where we go to

Let us realize that rose for each other

You have sat next to me long enough
Now is the time for you to come in
        . . . and sit in my heart

The conversation
        which is taking place between us
        cannot be expressed in words
The stories
        that are within us
        can only be shared in silence

No one will hear us
No one will separate us again
We no longer need to seek safety
This is a state of belonging

So come in
        . . . and sit in my heart

I am like the cup of wine
    which surrenders all that I contain
       with the touch of your lips

I am like that pearl
    which belongs to anyone
       who opens my heart

I am that fallen tree
    which will warm any heart
       who puts a spark in me

I am that ray of light
    that brings the vision of love
       into your eyes

I am a beggar who begs to give you love

I am a Sufi

I have come from love
I have brought great news

I am bearing roses, fruits and shade trees
I have brought kisses from unimaginable distances
I have brought tears of the Beloved
   to wash your feet clean
      of any dust of the past
I have brought musical instruments
   to put you to sleep at night
      and awaken you in the morning
I have brought you food
   that will give the taste of heaven

Finally
I have brought you breath
   right out of the Beloved's mouth

Let us hold hands
   and dissolve into this brilliant moment

Yes
   I have brought you

When you appeared in the doorway
    I thought that the sun itself
        had come to visit

Your brightness did not blind me
    It deepened me
My heart did not miss a beat to greet you

You may come and you may go
    It doesn't matter
When you walked in my door
    my cage was opened

I haven't been back since

A very brief glance of love
has made me a wanderer for the rest of my life

Come naked to my aloneness
    deep in the evening

Let us not be covered by any veils

I want to know you in your intensity
    which brings me back a life
        I have forgotten to live for

Come like a rose
    in absolute openness
        so we can dissolve in your golden heart

Come to me without anything
    so we can abandon everything
        to blend
            and to make the same fiber
                that will keep us together
                and together
                    and together

If you must go tonight . . . and leave me behind
    take this small package of love
        wrapped with my heart

If you must go tonight
    take my eyes with you
        so J can see your path
            and support every footstep of your travel
                with my soul

If you must go tonight
    please take my life with you
        for it is not worth living
            when J am left behind

But if you must go tonight . . . to be free
    then leave everything ~ everything behind

If you hear someone dancing
    in the middle of the night
And at dawn his eyes
    are full of morning dew
Then you know a lover is present

Dance with him
Cry with him

Make footsteps big enough
    for everyone to fit them
        and follow

Tonight is the wedding night

Tonight
    is the beginning of a never~ending lovemaking

Tonight
    when I drink a drop of you
        I become an ocean
    and when you dissolve in me
        you become the oceankeeper

After tonight
    nothing is left but to wave in each other

Love is like a wind

In a barren place
        you will not see the wind
But in a rose garden
        when a rose waves at you
            you know wind is present

When a message of a rose brushes your face
        you know the wind
            has brought you that fragrance

You may not see love now
        but there is a wind coming at you
So go to the rose garden
Feel that wind coming from every angle of life

Better yet
Be that rose
Let the wind shake you
        and carry your fragrance
            that sends the message of welcome
                to everyone who comes near you
Be at the mercy of the wind
Be that instrument of love

Take off your shoes
Where we are going
    you will not be touching the ground

Take off your hat
You will not need shade from the sun

Take off your mask
We know how beautiful you are inside

Please offer your silence
We do not need spoken words
    to blend

Just sing . . . if you can
Otherwise, hum-m-m

Do not look for anything
    that focuses you to a narrow path
Our path is wider than life

Don't wish for anything
You were born with all things

You need only one thing
And that is to step forward
    and be counted as one of us

I feel the strokes of your breath through me
Your music is painting this poor soul
     with the richest colors of the universe
My hunger is so intense
     I can engulf your whole being in an instant
And if you look at me just once
     I shall burn to my last essence
          to warm your feet

Until that moment of truth
     I shall walk toward you

You bring me to your lips like a flute
        yet forget to blow
How can I make music without your breath?

I want more than that
I want your soul blowing through me
I want your touch to feed my fire
I want your eyes to see my truth
I want everything you have and more
Is that too much to ask?

In this life
        there is nothing worth holding onto
In the other life
        there is nothing to own

Just you and me merging toward each other
Blow into me
Let the flute speak of this truth

Blow . . .

Stay for a while
I have not yet caught my breath
　　from the impact of looking at you

Don't be in such a hurry to leave
　　for if you do
　　　　my life would leave me to follow you

Don't stop singing
　　My inspiration and creativity ride on it

Keep touching me
　　That makes me live beyond this moment

I know a time will come
　　when I must leave my body
Then we will leave together

I hear something in the background of my life that says
　　'Please stay
　　　　We are making beautiful music together'

You taste one drop of an ocean
    you know the taste of the whole ocean

You taste a kiss from one lover
    you surrender to love your whole life

You see one sunset
    you fall in love with colors forever

On a starry night with full shining moon
    you become a part of the universe for eternity

I thought I knew

Then you came out of unknowing
I had to abandon everything
    to stand before you

Now I know what love is all about

Come to this street
    only with your fragrance

What you are or are not
    is not invited
What you say or don't say
    will not be heard

Only the music of your soul is needed

Come in
    as a melody
And when we become in tune
    then go on your way
        in harmony

I kiss your breath
    when you sing from your heart
I kiss your feet
    when you dance to the tune
        of impossible dreams
And I walk away
    when you talk of this or that of this world

If I do come back
I want to hear your pulse
    beating rhythm with the tune
        we were meant to be

Don't speak
Leave that to ordinary people

Hum to me with your heartbeat
I will hear everything you are made of

When you feel grace
    God is saying 'hello' to you

When you feel your heart can no longer hold you alone
    God is saying 'hello' to you

When your eyes are full of so many tears
    that nothing is visible
And you are so open that everything is possible
    God is saying 'hello' to you

When you see all the differences have turned into roses
    with fragrances that no one can deny
    God is saying 'hello' to you

When you are no longer alone
    even in the darkest corner of life
    God has become your companion

When you feel graceful
    and joy is pouring out of every cell of your existence
    God has become you

When you no longer can identify yourself
    with anything that exists
    You are now in union with God

This is the path of everyone who is alive
    and has an open heart to serve them
May you be served with that openness

By what right
    do you sit next to me
        when my heart has already invited you in?

By what right
    do you cry in a friend's doorway?

By what right
    do you crawl
        when your heart says 'Let's fly'?

The miracle that makes you breathe, love and dance
    will never give any right
        but to love and dance at every breath

There must be some sense to this loving
I have lost everything
      yet I am ecstatic

If there is any reason to this madness
      please ~ please do not tell me

In your silence
   I feel your pain
When you whisper
   I hear your shouts
In your tears
   I see the fire

Where do you come from?
Where are you going?

I want to sing the way you sing
   I want to cry the way you cry
      I want to feel pain the way you feel pain
        I want to go where you go
          I want to die the way you die
           I want . . .
            I want . . .
             I want . . .

Moon is closed tonight

You have to find love with your own light

The fire that burns my hand
    and leaves me with blisters?

        No, not that fire

The fire that comes to my home uninvited
    and leaves me with nothing but ashes?

        No, not that fire

The fire that burns my soul
    and frees me from all that I have become
    and purifies me of all existence
    and joins me in eternal flame

        That fire, I am looking for

That fire gives infinite freedom
    and all~consuming love
That fire which burns all that is not love

Yes, that fire
    ~ that friend ~
        I am looking for

Love has no form
   but it will form you

Love has no words
   but it will make you write poetry

Love has no life
   but it will give you a purpose to live

Love has no heat
   but it makes you burn from the moment of impact

Love has no feeling or mercy
   but it makes you feel everything to its ultimate
     with mercy

Love has no compassion
   but it makes you give up your life
     for a simple kiss, a touch, a tear or a song

Love is without form
   for it is unlimited

First time I looked at you
    you showed me your heart
First time I kissed you
    you burned my insides
First time I listened to you
    you touched my being
First time you caressed me
    I learned how to dance on the clouds
First time you asked me to love you
    I learned how to die
First time you said good~bye to me
    I learned how to laugh deeply
        for I knew I would never be far enough from you
          for the good~bye to take its meaning

Every day . . . we meet
Every hour . . . we meet
Every second . . . we meet

There is no time to separate
There is no place for good~byes
I know now
    not even death will take me away from you

Tonight I shall drop my veil
  as I stand before you
Should I drop my body as well
  before you take me?

Tonight I will leave life as I know it
  so you can enter me
Would I ever be the same?

Tonight I will give up all I have known
  to sit in your circle

Tonight I must give up life
  to get ready to learn the first lesson of love

Tonight is the night
  when the candle begins to burn **me**
    in order to create light

Tonight is a good night

I will go on living
That is not the proof of my existence

If I have raised a few roses here and there
That's the proof

Be aware
This is love calling

If I get a chance to crack your walls
        I will do so
If I am able to break into your cage and send you free
        I will do so
If I can take your heart out and send your soul home
        I will do so
If you fight me
        I will fight you back
If you love me
        I will love you back
If you run away
        I will run against you

The only way out is the way of home
When that happens
        you will find me in your heart
                welcoming you
Be aware
        for I could strike at any moment

You ask
　'Where is God?'

I say
　'Laugh deeply
　　　and you shall hear Him from within
　　　　　where the source of laughter exists'

A lover loves death

Every kiss must die
     to bring intense hunger
         for a new kiss
Every day must finish
     to meet a new dawn
Every tear must dry up
         to invite laughter

A creek
gently flowing among the pebbles
in the stream
whispering freshness
flowing through and around
whatever touches it

That's the teacher I'm looking for

Last hurricane
    took away everything I had

Next hurricane
    should stay longer
       and take me away too

We are happy even without wine
for we are well~drenched in each other

Why should I stay?

You came once
You took all
You left behind a dried~up kiss
    which I have been trying to water with tears
        to keep alive

Why should I stay this long?
Because you might come back

Take this pen from me
    before I write crazier things

They tell me I am spiritual
    but I see myself as a prostitute
I do anything for the price of love

Please take this damn pen away from me!

I tried to drown myself
    but kept coming up for air

So I lived

Now I drown myself in love
    and no amount of breathing
        will save me from this drowning

Be still
    even with the wind of the world
        seeking to bend you

Be still
    and let God's breath
        be the only breeze
            to move you

One night
I came upon some intoxicated darvishes
        so much in love
                that lover and Beloved were indistinguishable

I got closer to listen to their conversation
To my amazement
        they were trading moons and offering stars
                for a poem
                a wink
                or a single strand of long hair

So foolish they looked that I had to join them
They asked me if I had brought a moon for offering
I became foolish like they were
        so I said 'Yes'

Now I can proudly say
        I can offer the moon for a single smile

You are like bottled sunshine
        floating on the sea
                or planted in mud

Wherever this life places you
        you are still sunshine inside

Fill this heart
    that I might sing again
Warm my heart
    that I can love again
Take my mind
    that I will be free again
Take your sword and slice me open
    that I can cry again
Take me completely
    that I can be again
        be again . . . and be again
    that being which is one with you
       and none without you

One day
you will not need to pick flowers to feel fresh

Whatever is near will do

Hundreds of swords
    could not touch me

One eyelash from you
    cut me in half

Intoxicated as we are
    who will lead us home?

If we are as intoxicated as you say
    then we have packed our home in each other's heart
        knowing with this level of intoxication
            we will never find our way back

The only road we can see is what is ahead

Last night you came to see me in a dream . . .

Your velvet breath brushed my tears of separation
    like a breeze through a rose garden
My knees could no longer hold my weight
    and my heart could no longer control my laughter

Finally
    my soul came to greet us
Then
    with you and me indistinguishable
        we danced till nothing of us was
            anymore

If you're offered a rose from someone
    standing on the side of the road we travel
You should take the rose
    carry its essence
        and be grateful of the offering

If you choose to pluck the petals
    and let them fall beneath your feet
Every step of that path you walk on
    will be a step away from preciousness

If you don't walk with me in this small wedge of life
    I shall fall
        not knowing where I will land
In this fraction of time
    make love to me
        or I have been wasted unmercifully
Let me see you in this one time spark of light
    or these eyes were meant for nothing
Whisper to me for this one breath of life
    so I can say I have tasted life as it is meant to be

Take me
    for I am your fruit
Don't let me fall and rot
    for I am sweet~tasting
We are who we are
    and we are meant to serve each other
        in life
        in love
        and beyond

What a taste
What a moment
What a life
    in your presence

When someone says 'I love you'
     don't take the words
     take the lover

When someone offers you a kiss
     don't kiss their lips
     kiss their heart

When someone is shedding tears
     don't wipe them
     drink them

When someone reaches to touch you
     don't touch them
     put your heart in their hand

When someone walks away from you
     don't stand there
     walk with them

If you can do all of this
     you just might be a beginner of love

In this tear~stained world
　　all I wanted to do was to taste love
That taste was never far
　　but I could never reach it

Then you came along
　　and brought it close enough for my touch

Now I am more than hungry
I want to stay with you
　　with all that I am
　　　for the rest of my time

Put your lips on my lips
    and let your heart do the talking
Put your hand in my hand
    and let your soul do the ascending
Look into my eyes
    and see love has spread its wings
        to carry you
            to where the music of love is made

Walk with me
We are not going anywhere
    but practicing togetherness

And hold my hand
I feel closer this way

If anyone asks
Tell them I am in the garden
    listening to the roses
        and singing to the fallen leaves
            and directing traffic of the honey bees

The gauge of a love poem is
how deeply it fills your soul

or

how shallow your life becomes
without love

or

how quickly you give up everything
to hear a songbird

or

how long the sunset lasts
through the night

or

how easy it becomes
to kiss the pain good-bye

or

how quickly you say 'yes'
to everything that surrounds you

When you become the songs that your mother sang
    when she was holding you
Then you are fully grown

I have seen roses
How can my Springs ever be lonely?

I have heard you calling me
How can I ever lose the sight of music?

Ever since I smelled your aroma
        I have become hungry for the essence of life

They tell me
        love is that
My thirst tells me
        it is more than love
        It's the whole of creation itself

The essence of you is all that is

Hundreds of thieves
     cannot steal a single strand of love
        without falling in love

Thieves become lovers
     and lovers become thieves
That is the way of exchanging hearts

Tonight I will not sleep
I am tired of dreams
    that will not come true

Tonight I would like to play the music
    I was meant to be

Tonight I want to eat the world
    with my heart
        not with my mouth

Tonight I will travel the world
    to expose my secrets

Tonight is the night
    I will raise hell with Gods

Like a flute
    how can I sing
        without the touch of your lips

Like a flute
    I am lifeless
        without your breath blowing through me

Like a flute
    how can I change my tune
        without the caressing of your fingers

Like love
    how can I exist
        without dissolving in you

Out of nowhere
    you came with a dagger
        and stabbed me in my heart
You killed the dead and brought me life
Such an unmerciful act

For that
    I shall surrender my heart to you again and again
Such swords are made in Heaven
    and the blacksmith is the Beloved

Come in
Take a rest from the heat and the dusty road
You have been sailing this ship of life
    through the mysteries of nature
        and at the mercy of chances

Sit down
    and let me wash your feet
        and tell you stories to put your mind at rest

Let me pour some water with ice over your head
    so you can cool down your thoughts
Let me prepare you for your final journey
    which will be much longer than this one
Let me also prepare myself to be your disciple
    so J can also begin my last travel

Please come in from the heat and dust
You have come so far
    and J have waited all my life to receive you
        even for a moment

Here's the cool water . . .
Here's my life . . .
Take them both . . .

In my temple there is a seat
that is the throne of love
Come in!

There is a no need to kneel or pray
Just dance!
Dance to the tune of silence
Sing without sound

When you are tuned like the finest musical instrument
leave this temple
and play your music
to all who come near you

I borrowed some light from the sun
    some love from the moon
    and some wisdom from life

I borrowed some tears from a lover
    and laughter from a friend

I also borrowed some gentleness from a rose

I borrowed some wildness from a newborn goat
    to roam free in every direction
        like the waves of the ocean

I did all of that to get ready for a picnic
    to invite you to this feast of life
        with all its members present

From tears to the ocean
From the newborn to the sun
From smiles and open hearts
    I invite everyone to this picnic
        to be the participants

Let us dance while this lasts
Let us feast on each other while we're alive
Let us leave the same for the ones
    who will arrive after us

Don't be the only one in the coming Spring
not flowering

Made in the USA
Lexington, KY
05 December 2014